The Three Laws of Motion

by Tara Funk

Table of Contents

Introduction

Some objects move. Moving objects are in **motion**. We see objects in motion everywhere.

Isaac Newton was a scientist. Isaac Newton wrote **laws** about motion. Read about the three laws of motion.

▲ We use the laws of motion.

▲ Isaac Newton

action

direction

forces

friction

inertia

Isaac Newton

PHILOSOPHIÆ
NATURALIS
PRINCIPIA

laws

motion

reaction

speed

See the Glossary on page 30.

3

What Are Newton's Three Laws of Motion?

Isaac Newton wrote the laws of motion. Newton's laws tell about **forces** and motion. A push is a force. A pull is a force.

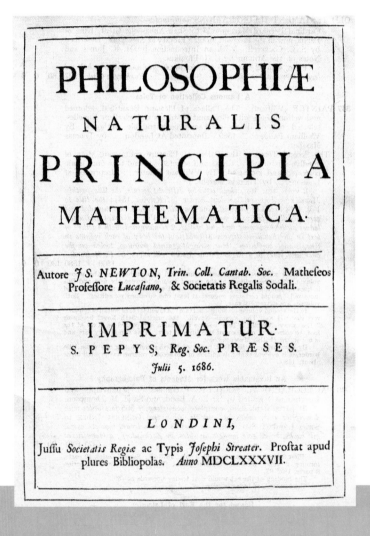

PHILOSOPHIÆ

NATURALIS

PRINCIPIA

MATHEMATICA.

Autore JS. NEWTON, Trin. Coll. Cantab. Soc. Matheseos Professore Lucasiano, & Societatis Regalis Sodali.

IMPRIMATUR·

S. PEPYS, Reg. Soc. PRÆSES.

Julii 5. 1686.

LONDINI,

Jussu Societatis Regiæ ac Typis Josephi Streater. Prostat apud plures Bibliopolas. Anno MDCLXXXVII.

▲ Newton's book told about his laws.

The laws of motion tell how things happen.
The laws of motion tell why things happen.

▲ **These runners are in motion.**

The first law tells what causes motion. The first law tells what stops motion.

▲ A kick causes motion.
The soccer ball is in motion.

The first law of motion:

Objects at rest stay at rest. Objects in motion stay in motion. A force causes motion. A force stops motion.

The second law of motion tells about **speed**. Speed is how fast the motion is. The same law tells about **direction**. Direction is the path of motion.

▲ Speed is important in car races.

The second law of motion:

Stronger forces cause faster motion. Heavier objects need more force to cause motion. Forces cause motion to change direction.

▲ **Forces cause the car to move faster.**

The third law tells about **action** and **reaction**. Objects in motion cause more motion.

▲ The gas pushing down is an action.

▲ The shuttle pushing up is a reaction.

The swimmer pushes the water backward. The water pushes the swimmer forward. The push backward is an action. The push forward is a reaction.

The third law of motion:

The force of an action equals the force of a reaction.

▲ Swimmers use the third law of motion.

TRY THIS

You can show the third law of motion.
1. Blow up a balloon.
2. Let the balloon go.
3. Air leaves the balloon. Air leaving the balloon is action.
4. The balloon moves backward. The balloon moving backward is reaction.

Chapter 2

How Do We Use the Three Laws in Sports?

What sports do you like to play? Do you play baseball? Do you play hockey? Do you swim? Do you play golf? We use the laws of motion in sports.

We see motion in many sports. We feel the laws of motion in many sports. The laws of motion help us play better. The laws of motion make sports more fun.

A skier uses the laws of motion. A skier uses force to start motion. Motion starts when the skier leans forward.

▲ **This skier is starting to move down the mountain.**

Turning is part of skiing. A skier uses force to make a turn. The skier bends at the knees. The skis dig into the snow. The skier turns down the mountain.

FIGURE IT OUT

What laws of motion does a skier use?

▲ Force helps the skier turn.

We see the laws in cycling. Some helmets help cyclists go faster. People who make helmets know the laws of motion. Some bicycles help cyclists go faster. People who make bicycles know the laws of motion.

▲ These bicycles do not weigh very much. These bicycles help the cyclists go faster.

The fastest bicycles do not weigh very much. The fastest cyclists have these bicycles. Cyclists need less force to move these bicycles. The bicycles have thin tires. The thin tires help the cyclists move faster.

DID YOU KNOW?

The fastest speed on a bicycle was 127 miles per hour (204 kilometers per hour).

▲ These cyclists use the laws of motion to go fast.

Hockey players use the laws of motion. A force moves a hockey puck. Players hit the hockey puck. The hit is a force. What stops the motion of the puck?

▲ Hockey players use the laws of motion.

A force stops the motion of the puck. **Friction** is a force. Friction is rubbing. The puck rubs on the ice. The puck stops.

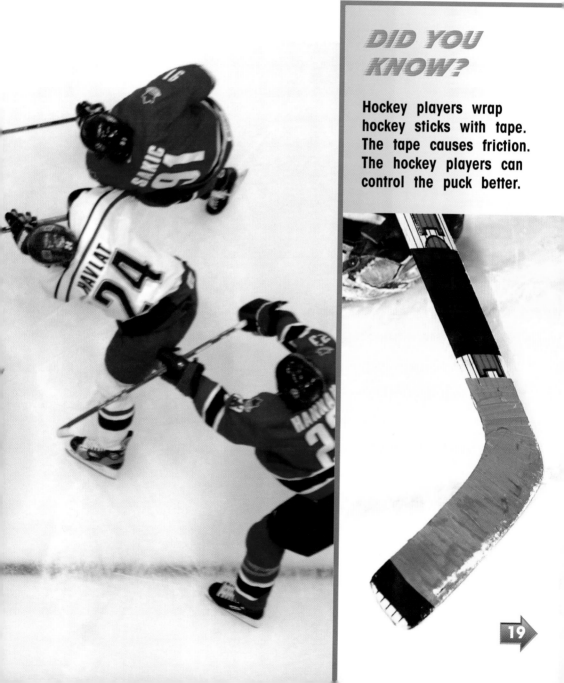

DID YOU KNOW?

Hockey players wrap hockey sticks with tape. The tape causes friction. The hockey players can control the puck better.

How Do We Use the Three Laws to Make Cars?

People who make cars know the laws of motion. People use what they know to make cars fast. People use what they know to make cars safe.

▲ This car is very fast. This driver is safe.

Cars need seat belts because of **inertia**. Inertia keeps an object in motion. Inertia keeps your body in motion. Your body stays in motion when a car stops. The seat belt stops the motion of your body. The first law of motion is the law of inertia.

▲ People who make cars understand inertia.

THEN AND NOW

The first cars did not have seat belts. Now we have laws about seat belts. All cars must have seat belts.

Car makers use the laws of motion. Car makers use the laws to keep people safe. Sometimes cars crash. People can get hurt. Some people stay alive because car makers know about motion.

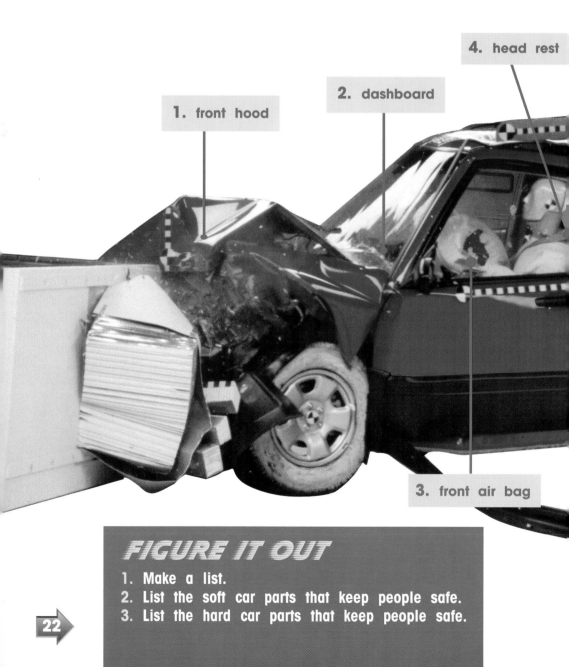

4. head rest

2. dashboard

1. front hood

3. front air bag

FIGURE IT OUT

1. Make a list.
2. List the soft car parts that keep people safe.
3. List the hard car parts that keep people safe.

Cars have soft parts to keep people safe.
Cars have hard parts to keep people safe.

5. side door

6. body

7. tire

1. front hood **The front of the car folds up in a crash.**

2. dashboard **Soft parts absorb force. Soft parts cover sharp parts.**

3. front air bag **Air bags stop people from hitting hard car parts. Air bags help stop people in motion.**

4. head rest **Head rests stop the motion of people's heads.**

5. side door **Soft parts in the door absorb force.**

6. body **A metal cage surrounds people. The cage absorbs force in a crash.**

7. tires **Tires rub against the road. The rubbing stops the car.**

Where Do We See the Three Laws in Nature?

We see fish swim through water. The fish are in motion. The fish push the water back. The water pushes the fish forward.

▲ We see the laws of motion when fish swim.

We see birds fly through the air. The birds are in motion. The birds push the air down. The air pushes the birds up.

FIGURE IT OUT

Which laws of motion do we see when birds fly?

▲ We see the laws of motion when birds fly.

We see rock slides in nature. We see rocks rolling down a mountain. The rocks were not moving. A force caused the rocks to roll down the mountain.

▲ The rocks stay in motion until a force stops the motion.

Rock slides can be dangerous. People try to stop rock slides. People put fences near mountain roads. The fences stop the motion of rocks. The rocks cannot hit cars and people.

▲ The fence stops the motion of rocks.

Summary

Isaac Newton wrote three laws of motion. We see the laws of motion everywhere. We use the laws of motion to play. We use the laws of motion to stay safe.

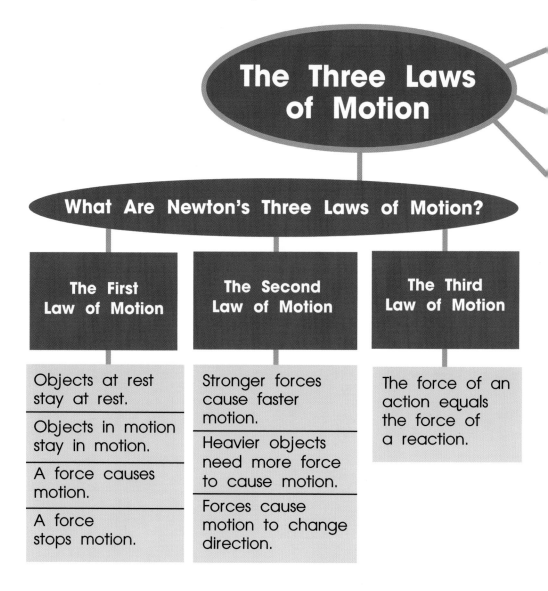

The Three Laws of Motion

What Are Newton's Three Laws of Motion?

The First Law of Motion	The Second Law of Motion	The Third Law of Motion
Objects at rest stay at rest.	Stronger forces cause faster motion.	The force of an action equals the force of a reaction.
Objects in motion stay in motion.	Heavier objects need more force to cause motion.	
A force causes motion.	Forces cause motion to change direction.	
A force stops motion.		